DAM
Beaver

Tree Frog

Sloth

Koala

Monkey

TREE DWELLERS

Dugong

Alligator

Salamander

Fish

Hippopotamus

Sea Otter

WATER DWELLERS

WEB
Spider

T0006460

The story you are about to read is *mostly* true.
Please note, many animals have homes with specific
names. For instance, a bower and a drey are both
a *type* of nest. And some, but not *all*, porcupines
make their dens in trees. Additionally, some animals
burrow *and* nest—and this is double duty.

Hence, the characters in this book would like
proper credit for their hard work.

For Kevin —MF

For Perley James and Betts —BJS

I Live in a Tree Trunk
Text copyright © 2023 by Meg Fleming
Illustrations copyright © 2023 by Brandon James Scott
All rights reserved. Manufactured in Italy.
No part of this book may be used or reproduced in any manner whatsoever without
written permission except in the case of brief quotations embodied in critical articles
and reviews. For information address HarperCollins Children's Books, a division of
HarperCollins Publishers, 195 Broadway, New York, NY 10007.
www.harpercollinschildrens.com

Library of Congress Control Number: 2022930785
ISBN 978-0-06-320521-5

The artist used Adobe Photoshop to create the digital illustrations for this book.
Typography by Chelsea C. Donaldson
23 24 25 26 27 RTLO 10 9 8 7 6 5 4 3 2 1
❖
First Edition

I LIVE IN A TREE TRUNK

WORDS BY **Meg Fleming**

PICTURES BY **Brandon James Scott**

HARPER

An Imprint of HarperCollinsPublishers

I live in a tree trunk.

I live in a barn.

I live in a bog.

I live in a mound.

My place is a burrow
hidden in the ground.

Are you for SURE?
I had NO clue!

Mine's a burrow, too.

I live in a hedgerow.

I live in a drey.

I live in a coral reef.

I live on the bay.

I live in a web.

(Tell me you're impressed.)

My place is a stable.

My place is a nest.

Are you for SURE?
I had NO clue!

Mine's a nest!

Mine's a nest.

Mine's a nest, too!

I live in a hive
and dine out in a flower.

I ramble in a bramble.

I shower in a bower.

I live in a desert.

I live on a ranch.

My place is an iceberg.

My place is a branch.

Are you for SURE?
I had NO clue!

Mine's a branch!

Mine's a branch.

Mine's a branch, too.

I live in a riverbed.

I live on a bank.

I lived in a chimney, once.

I live in a tank.

I live in a pigsty!

I live in a pen.

My place is a dam.

My place is a den.

Are you for SURE?
I had NO clue!

Mine's a den.

Mine's a den!

Mine's a den, too!

I live in a coop.

I live in a lodge.

I live on a soccer field.

I'm in your garage.

I'm out in the yard.

I'm out in a shed.

When it's time for sleeping,
my place is . . .

YOUR BED!

Mine's a bed!

Mine's a bed!

Mine's a bed, too!

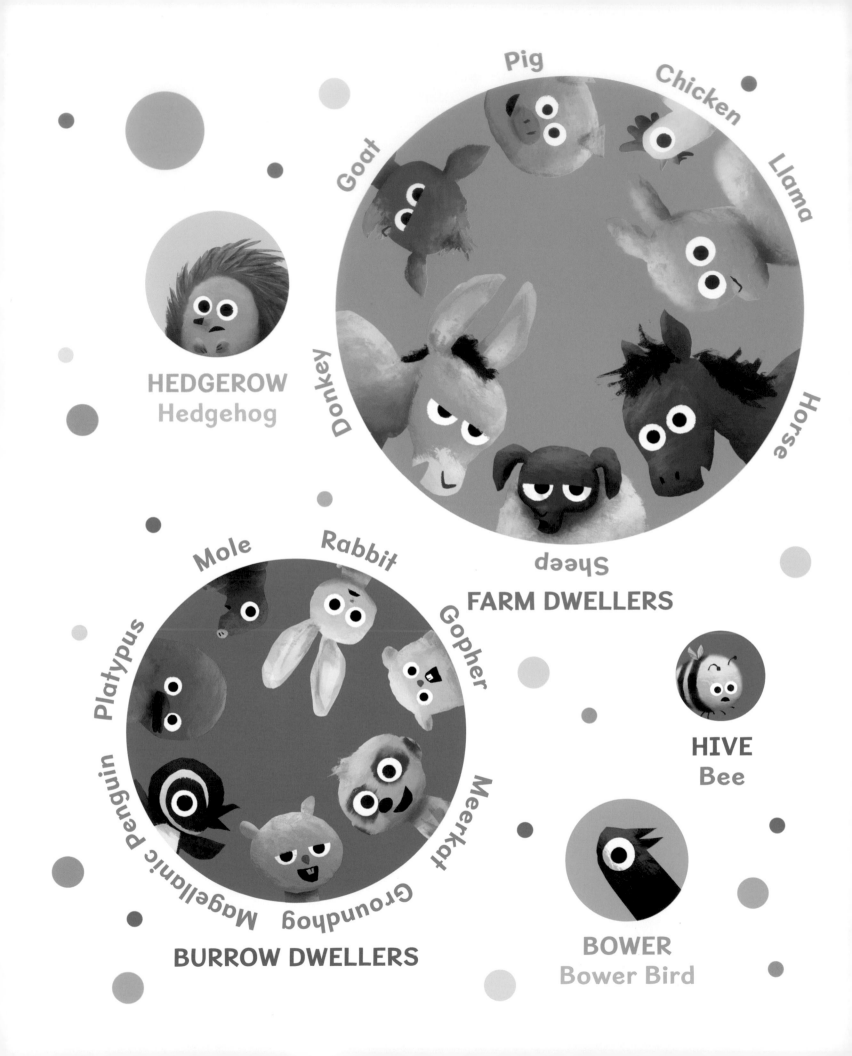

HEDGEROW
Hedgehog

Pig
Goat
Chicken
Llama
Donkey
Horse
Sheep

FARM DWELLERS

Mole
Rabbit
Platypus
Gopher
Magellanic Penguin
Groundhog
Meerkat

BURROW DWELLERS

HIVE
Bee

BOWER
Bower Bird